Tanya

Ashley Tudor
Leah Holcomb
Morgan Mann
c/o 2003

Sum 2001

Touch
My
Heart

in Summer

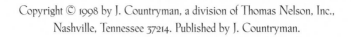

Contents

Summer

WEEK 1

Summertime Exercise
Roses in a Clay Pot
Too Much Flour
Delighting to Do God's Will
Take One More Step
Rest and Relaxation

Summer

WEEK 2

The "Ropes Course" of Life
God's Gifts for Today
Give Me More Time, Lord
Lessons About Worry
The White–Winged Swan of Summer
God's Grand Designs

Summer

WEEK 3

God's Strong Women
Laughing at Loads
A Place by the River
God's Curriculum
Let Joy Invade Your Heart
A Place of Quiet Rest

Summer

WEEK 4

Our Minutes Are Holy
The Somewhere Woman
Plantings of the Heart
Think of God's Love
God—the Source of All Security
Bone–Deep Honesty

Summer

WEEK 5

Sloshing Annoyances
Taking Little Steps
There Be Dragons Here
God Blesses a Thankful Heart
Christmas in the Summertime
Quiet in God

Summer

WEEK 6

God Sets the Boundaries
Nesting in God's Love
Life is for Loving
Stargazing
Glad Is Great
Attached to the Fixed Point

Summer

WEEK 7

The Best Part Is Getting There
A New Beginning
Life–Giving Power
Deep Roots Endure
Time for Beauty
What Jesus Stood For

Summer

WEEK 8

A Tiny Seed of Faith
Listening for God's Voice
Knowing God's Will
Freedom from Anxiety
"Soft" Times for the Soul
Trust God and Be Quiet

Summer

WEEK 9

A Heavenly Catalog
Moments Wrapped in Ribbon
The Heart's True Home
Love Works Hard
Faith and Power Go Hand in Hand
The Task of a Lifetime

Summer

WEEK 10

God's Teaching Tools
Living a Creative Life
Fear Not, Fret Not
Walk Straight and Tall
There Will Always Be Two
Safe and Secure

Summer

WEEK 11

The Blessing of Daily Bread
Our Savior Shepherd
Mary's Gift
The Dignity of a Godly Woman
Paint, Or Get Off the Ladder
God Always Answers Prayer

Summer

WEEK 12

Pickles and Preservatives
My Portion and My Cup
Simple Solitude
Bumps and Jolts Along the Way
Lord, Keep Me At It
Tending the Inner Garden

Summer

WEEK 13

Singing Birds of the Heart
Everyday Blessings
Christ Redeems the Crummy Stuff
In the Living Room of God's Heart
An Ordinary Path
The Seasons of God's Care

ACKNOWLEDGMENTS

The day was as balmy as summer, and we felt like butterflies after
a frost, and fluttered about, enjoying the sunshine all day.

LOUISA MAY ALCOTT

Flowers are like children.
Someone needs to be their keeper.

INGRID
TROBISCH

Keeper of
the Springs

Summertime Exercise

✺

My heart is overflowing with a good theme;
. . . my tongue is the pen of a ready writer.

Psalm 45:1

*I*f ever there is a blessing–time of year, it is in late summer when all the joys of our work pile up their bountiful rewards. . . . I think of what my mother called her blessing song: "When Upon Life's Billows." . . . She often sang the lyrics as she hurried about baking fat lemon pies or spading her garden where she taught onions and petunias to live together peaceful: *"Count your blessings—name them one by one; Count your blessings— see what God has done."* . . .

Do you count your blessings daily? If not, it's the best exercise there is! How high can you count? It's sure to surprise you what the Lord does for you daily. I am sure I have more blessings than any other person alive!

JUNE
MASTERS
BACHER
Quiet Moments
for Women

God is God, and we must never reduce Him to anything less.

EDITH
SCHAEFFER

✺

Week 1

*The sweetness of life lies
in usefulness, like honey
deep in the heart of
a clover bloom.*

LAURA INGALLS
WILDER

Roses in a Clay Pot

✳

But you are a chosen generation, a royal priesthood,
a holy nation, His own special people.

1 Peter 2:9

I have two containers for flowers. One is an old clay pot, the other is a beautiful cut–glass vase. Occasionally, I receive a lovely bouquet of roses. If I put them in the vase, the glory is shared. If I put them in the pot, attention is drawn to the blossoms. "What beautiful flowers!" exclaim my visitors, ignoring the container.

God chooses such earthen vessels that his glory may be better displayed. In fact, he has told us that he will not share his glory with another. He insists on receiving the honor due his name.

Sometimes I want to be the cut–glass vase and draw attention to myself. I have to be reminded that my sense of importance lies in the miracle of God's choosing me. He placed his roses in my vase. In this lies my value. What use is a vase without flowers?

Halo my path with gentleness and love.

PURITAN
PRAYER

J I L L   B R I S C O E
Quiet Times with God

Too Much Flour

That I may know Him and the power of His resurrection,
and the fellowship of His sufferings.
Philippians 3:10

One way of looking at the mix of the parts of ourselves is to picture the facets of our personalities as ingredients of a pie, dumped in a bowl in what we hope are pleasing proportions, but maybe not. Maybe our subconscious is so heavy with unworked–through material, it clogs the recipe with too much flour. Our hopes and dreams and egos are tossed in a bowl and stirred by life, and sometimes that's exactly what it feels like—being tossed and stirred by life. But in order to become a real pie, we need to be stirred. We also need to be cooked, and God's love in this analogy is like the heat necessary for us to blend together into the person God wants us to become. If God did not allow life to stir us up, and if He did not allow us to "feel the heat," we would remain a lumpy mass of disparate ingredients. God's love is the catalyst to change raw materials into a delectable treat.

The peace that passes understanding, then, is what we feel when we're being lifted gingerly, carefully out of the oven, displayed as a masterpiece. We have become whole. The ingredients of our lives have become integrated. Only then are we ready to be used to feed others.

LESLIE WILLIAMS
Night Wrestling

Delighting to Do God's Will

---- ✳ ----

Love one another fervently with a pure heart.

1 P e t e r 1 : 2 2

G od could have chosen to do everything Himself, but instead He so conceived the world that birds must build nests and sit on eggs, . . . bees must construct honeycombs, and man must will and work.

It is the willingness we must emphasize here. We pray "Thy will be done on earth *as it is in heaven.*" God's will is always *willingly* and *gladly* done in heaven. Willing obedience is a very different thing from coercion. A college dean once observed that the happiest students on any campus are the musicians and athletes. "Why?" I asked. "Because they're disciplined, and they volunteered to be disciplined." People sitting in required lectures are under discipline, and people sitting in the television lounge are "volunteers," but athletes and musicians put themselves under a coach or director who tells them what to do. They delight to do his will. They are actually having fun.

God does not coerce us to follow Him. He invites us.

> *We love God by loving our neighbor, and we can love our neighbor only as we love God.*
>
> RICHARD FOSTER
>
> ✳

ELISABETH ELLIOT
Discipline: The Glad Surrender

Like sunshine over a valley,
God's great love spreads out
over the whole earth.
J. HEINRICH
ARNOLD

Take One More Step

✳

We are in Him who is true, in His Son Jesus Christ.

1 John 5:20:

God's gift of faith and power are always adequate, no matter how desperate our situation has become. Exhaustion, frustration, tragedy may have us burdened down so that we despair of ever being free again. The pain may be unrelenting, the loss overwhelming, the loneliness damning. But God's power is great enough for our deepest desperation.

You can go on. You can pick up the pieces and start anew. You can face your fears. You can find peace in the rubble. You can have courage. There is healing for your soul.

My pastor gave an illustration that is the perfect picture of faith: You approach the closed door and wonder how you can get the door open with your arms so full of baggage. How, indeed? All that is necessary is to take one more step. The doors open automatically. . . .

Do you see? Take just one more step and you will be given the faith and the power to add another step, and another.

God is never away off somewhere else, He is always there.

OSWALD
CHAMBERS

✳

SUZANNE DALE EZELL
Living Simply in God's Abundance

Notes

Lord, we are rivers running to thy sea,
Our waves and ripples all derived from thee;
A nothing we should have, a nothing be,
Except for thee.

C H R I S T I N A   R O S S E T T I

(1 8 3 0 — 1 8 9 4)

Rest and Relaxation

And on the seventh day God ended His work . . .
and He rested on the seventh day.
GENESIS 2:2

God worked very hard for six days and then stopped his labor to relax and luxuriate in what he had done. . . .

The Israelite who observed God's Sabbath was doing what God was doing—he was resting because God had done all his work for him. There wasn't anything left to do.

Israel's Sabbath was essentially a test of faith in God's provision. . . . In the busiest times of the year, when hard workers thought they ought to work harder, God wouldn't let them work every day. They had to rest and rely on God's activity. By so doing they learned that even when they weren't working, things were getting done.

It's hard to rest when there's so much to be done, but God wanted his people to know that resting is one of the most important things human beings can do.

Resting in God is what
trusting in God feels like.

HARRIET
CROSBY

DAVID ROPER
Elijah: A Man Like Us

Open my heart, Lord,
to small daily things;
Each blessing You've shaped
that blossoms and sings.

JUNE MASTERS
BACHER

The "Ropes Course" of Life

✳

Eye has not seen, nor ear heard . . . the things which
God has prepared for those who love Him.

1 Corinthians 2:9

An acquaintance of mine recently signed up at a nearby university for a weekend "ropes course." The students arrive in the morning, are strapped into a harness, and spend the day climbing ropes to incredible heights.

It sounded perfectly horrible to me, but she was looking forward to it.

"When I face my fears—in this case, claustrophobia and fear of heights and overcome them, I feel better about myself," she said. . . . "It's wonderful . . . really."

I wasn't quite convinced. But I understand the principle. Going through the challenge is more fulfilling than finding a way around it.

You think you can never do it. . . . But once you're on the other side, you find yourself looking at the situation with different eyes. You see in a different light.

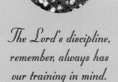

The Lord's discipline, remember, always has our training in mind.

WAYNE
JACOBSEN

✳

Week 2

PENELOPE J. STOKES
Faith: The Substance of Things Unseen

God's Gifts for Today

✳

*Who has known the mind of the Lord that he may
instruct Him? But we have the mind of Christ.*

1 Corinthians 2:16

[G]od] made us human. He made us to need what
he gives. He tells us to ask for it. Bread or
something like it is the most basic human
need. But I think we may include all human needs
under this heading. Guidance is one of them.

I like to picture the Lord handing me a platter at
the beginning of each new day. On it are the
things he has chosen as best for me, and my
prayer for daily bread is answered. My part is to
receive whatever he gives. Guidance for a decision
that need not be final until next Wednesday may
require one small move or commitment today. I accept
that and act on it without haggling with God because he
has not yet granted me all the information I am itching for.
Perhaps *patience* is his gift of bread for today or quietness, or the
gift of uncertainty that I may rest in his love, confident that when
the time is ripe, the guidance will be clear.

*We may not see the path,
but the One who leads
us knows the way.*

PENELOPE
J. STOKES

ELISABETH ELLIOT
God's Guidance

Give Me More Time, Lord

✳

Let us therefore come boldly to the throne of grace, that we may obtain mercy and find grace to help in time of need.

Hebrews 4:16

My friend Anne said that when she faced horrendous list days, she flat-out prayed for time. To her amazement and gratitude, the Lord often honored her prayer in unexpected ways. For instance, she'd be standing tenth in line at the grocery store with a cart piled high, and suddenly a new check-out stand would open up and the checker would come to her. Or, she would "coincidentally" run into people on her long list of phone calls, thus saving her much time.

God is interested in the texture of our days. One thing I've come to accept is that some days are busier than others; if we choose to participate in life, we cannot avoid this ebb and flow. On the flow days, when urgency drives us and we lurch (late) from one event to the next, we can pray for time like Anne. And God will give us little corners to cut so we don't have to be so breathless.

LESLIE WILLIAMS
Seduction of the Lesser Gods

Lessons About Worry

✳

He who is in you is greater than he who is in the world.

1   J o h n   4 : 4

When I was a little girl, I worried my shoes would shrink. After all, I had heard my teacher say my sandals were getting too small. When I was a teenager, I worried that I wouldn't get a date. When I got engaged, I worried I might be in a car wreck the eve of my wedding. When I had my first baby, I worried he would fall into the washing machine and drown! . . .

Being a graduated worrier I have had to learn some hard lessons about what worry does to me—and my family! Worry does not empty tomorrow of its problems; it simply empties today of its strength.

But more important, worry betrays a lack of trust in God's care and is really an unconscious blasphemy of him. . . . Lack of trust in God, the seedbed of worry, is sin! Now I can do something about that. I can repent of it and be determined to sin no more! My God delights to lend his strength to such resolve. "Trust me," he says. "Don't worry about anything."

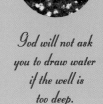

God will not ask you to draw water if the well is too deep.

MACDUFF

✳

JILL BRISCOE
Quiet Times with God

I love to listen to the
bird songs every day
And hear the free winds
whisper in their play,
Among the tall old trees
and sweet wild flowers.

LAURA INGALLS
WILDER

The White-Winged Swan of Summer

✸

Blessed are those who keep His testimonies,
who seek Him with the whole heart.

Psalm 119:2

The arrival and departure of a season is often unexpected or rather surprising. If we found a season one place last year, we look in vain to find it there the next. . . . One day it is the chirping sparrow of spring; the next, it is the graceful white–winged swan of summer. . . .

The world is wet with April's rain and dusky with May's purple lilacs; and sometimes there is no sign of the first June rose. But soon the month will set itself on course. Dawns will come fresh and sweet; noons will sparkle in tranquility; and twilights will bring baskets of sudden bloom. Unpredictable as summer's arrival may be, we know with a certain certainty that it will be here because God has given us His promise of the cycle of the seasons. We accept this promise as we accept all the other good promises He makes, both in this world and the world to come. This we do because of faith.

The highway of holiness is along the commonest road of life.

MARK GUY
PEARSE

JUNE MASTERS BACHER
Quiet Moments for Women

Notes

Earth's crammed with heaven,
And every common bush afire with God;
But only he who sees takes off his shoes;
The rest sit round it and pluck blackberries.

ELIZABETH BARRETT
BROWNING

God's Grand Designs

✳

*Be ye doers of the word, and not hearers
only, deceiving yourselves.*

James 1:22

The beach does not cover itself. It is covered
by the sea.

The shore does not change itself. It is shaped
by the tides.

The sea edge does not diminish its own size. The
ocean does this as it sweeps in upon it.

The alterations and rearrangements of the coast
are the eternal work of the eternal tides.

And in my life as one who lies open, exposed and
receptive to the action of The Most High, it is He
who will cover and conform me to His own pattern of
ultimate perfection. He does not relent, He does not
rest. He neither slumbers nor sleeps. It is He who is at
work upon my soul and within my spirit both to will and to do
according to His own grand designs.

*Religion may be learned
on Sunday, but it is lived
in the weekday's work.*

JOHN
DOUGHTY

W. PHILLIP KELLER
Songs of My Soul

I like to pray surrounded by the sight and smell of thriving herbs and flowers that assure me of God's faithfulness.

HARRIET CROSBY

God's Strong Women

✳

*Anxiety in the heart . . . causes depression,
but a good word makes it glad.*

Proverbs 12:25

Strong women intrigue me. I enjoy watching them organize large fund-raisers that make life better for less fortunate individuals. I admire parenting skills that strong women use; they work carefully to empower their children and help them grow strong. . . . The world is a good place because of sensitive, strong women.

But when is strength really a weakness? I have to admit that when it comes to the big decisions of life, trusting God is not my first line of thought. Instinctively I look within myself for answers. . . .

How often I make my plans and ask for God's blessing on my plan. Then with jaw set I move ahead thinking that my will is His will. Which finds me, again and again, needing to return to my point of departure and seek His wisdom on the front end of a decision....

Trusting God does not make me less of a women; it doesn't compromise my personality as a strong women. Depending on Him celebrates the wonderful, miraculous gift He has entrusted to me. Trusting Him is my strength.

> *True prayer is not asking God for what we want, but for what He wants.*
>
> J. OSWALD
> SANDERS
>
> ✳

SUZANNE DALE EZELL
Living Simply in God's Abundance

Week 3

That summer, lying in the long grass with my head propped against the back of a saddle, . . . I listened to the mountain silence until I could hear as far into it as the faintest clink of a cowbell.

EUDORA WELTY

One Writer's Beginnings

Laughing at Loads

✳

A merry heart makes a cheerful countenance,
but by sorrow of the heart the spirit is broken.

Proverbs 15:13

A smile on your heart means a smile on your face. Some people wear their hearts on their sleeves. What goes on inside, shows up outside. Have you ever asked a junior high daughter to help you with the housework? Her face tells the story. Her heart is definitely not in it!

When your heart has Jesus as its guest, it smiles. How can it do anything else? When your heart houses the one who is our joy, it cannot help grinning at grief, laughing at loads, and smiling at sorrows. Even when we are called to suffer, we cannot be sad or sour because we discover that we have been saved to sing. . . .

"But" you may object, "how can I even smile when I'm suffering, much less sing about it?" Look at Jesus! Can you look at Jesus and remain sober? When I'm in trouble, and I meet him in the secret place and he smiles at me, that mends my heart so I can mend others. He sets my heart singing.

JILL BRISCOE
Quiet Times with God

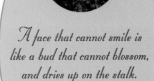

A face that cannot smile is
like a bud that cannot blossom,
and dries up on the stalk.

ANNA
WHITE

✳

A Place by the River

✳

In the time of trouble He shall hide me in His pavilion.

Psalm 27:5

When [my husband] gave up his secure job as a lawyer to go to seminary and we moved from our honeymoon home nestled among live oaks in Austin, I told him, "I'll give up a big house and financial security and a swimming pool, but I'm not giving up my dream for a place by the river." Throughout my rocky teenage years, I had returned summer after summer to the Texas hill country, with its smell of juniper, fresh grass, and cypress-lined rivers. In my adult life, a place by the river in the Texas hill country symbolized stability for me. Every time we moved, my heart kindled anew for a place by the river. . . .

After Stockton and I had trekked around the state serving various churches, I finally realized that my yearning for the place on the river was really a yearning for God. The Texas hill country—though a beautiful and special place—is really just another dot on the map. The desire for home goes much deeper, and God calls us to Him through our longing for a secure place here on earth. We can tramp all over the world searching for a place to call home; and yet all along, we carry home inside us, accesssible at all times through prayer.

LESLIE WILLIAMS
Seduction of the Lesser Gods

God's Curriculum

✳

*This Book of the Law shall not depart from your mouth,
but you shall meditate in it day and night.*

Joshua 1:8

There is a philosophy of secular education which holds that the student ought to be allowed to assemble his own curriculum according to his preferences. Few students have a strong basis for making these choices, not knowing how little they know. Ideas of what they need to learn are not only greatly limited but greatly distorted. What they need is *help*—from those who know more than they do.

Mercifully, God does not leave us to choose our own curriculum. . . . With intimate under-standing of our deepest needs and individual capaci-ties, He chooses our curriculum. We need only ask, "Give us this day our daily bread, our daily lessons, our homework." An angry retort from someone may be just the occasion we need in which to learn not only longsuffering and forgiveness, but meekness and gentleness; fruits not born in us but borne only by the Spirit.

Where do you begin in your search for wisdom? Begin with God.

LARRY LEA

ELISABETH ELLIOT
Keep a Quiet Heart

Life is so richly laden
a tree that it's almost
impossible to reach
out to pluck an apple
without getting baskets
full to overflowing.

MARJORIE
HOLMES

Let Joy Invade Your Heart

❋

Blessed are the people who know the joyful sound!

Psalm 89:15

How long has it been since you:

➤ Read a good book . . . wrote a poem . . . sang aloud? . . .

➤ Took painting lessons or played the piano? . . .

➤ Stopped at a roadside stand, bought an apple, polished it with the palm of your hand, and ate it right there?

➤ Removed the phone from the hook, filled the tub to brimming with bubble bath, and "soaked in" some of your favorite psalms of praise until the water cooled? . . .

➤ Greeted a stranger with a smile... praised a child...

How long, then, has it been since you felt that God was in control? He wants joy to invade our hearts and take over completely.

All of life is a gift, and God has given it for joy.

TERRY
LINDVALL

❋

JUNE MASTERS BACHER
The Quiet Heart

Notes

As the sun is full of light,
The ocean full of water,
Heaven full of glory,
So may my heart be full of thee.

PURITAN PRAYER

A Place of Quiet Rest

✳

May the Lord of peace Himself give you peace always in every way.

2   T h e s s a l o n i a n s   3 : 16

An old hymn came powerfully to mind as I faced into the birth of our third child after an urgent, eleventh-hour flight to Pennsylvania from Yugoslavia: "Jesus, I am resting, resting in the joy of what thou art. I am finding out the greatness of thy loving heart."

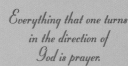

An attitude of rest. In a day when no matter who you talk to there *is never* enough time, cultivating an attitude of rest is the only way to survive the pressures with any semblance of serenity. Gone are the days of childhood abandon. The web of obligations, responsibilities, expectations is woven so tightly that we never cut loose and jump with effortless exuberance into the arms of our mother. Gone are the leisurely mornings when we sank deeper into the pillow's softness because we were home at last. But there is the voice of one who said, "Come to me all you who are weary and burdened, and I will give you rest" (Matthew 11:28 NIV).

Everything that one turns in the direction of God is prayer.

IGNATIUS
OF LOYOLA

✳

SARA   WENGER   SHANK
Coming Home

Summer is the time
when you take your
shoes off as often as
possible, leave work
as early as possible,
and head for the lake
or beach as soon as
possible.

**BERNIE
SHEAHAN**

Soul Searching

Our Minutes Are Holy

✷

God has sent His only begotten Son into the
world, that we might live through Him.

1 John 4:9

*L*ife is holy. Our days, our hours, our minutes are holy, created by God according to His holy purpose. The Bible begins with a beautiful, poetic account of how and what God created. He made a special place. He made it self-contained and filled it with His wonders. Then He gave male and female dominion over it all.

God loved the world and all the creatures He put here. In fact, He loved it so much, He decided to come and dwell here, to walk among the people, to dwell in the countrysides and to visit the lakes and mountains. . . . God revealed Himself in the ordinary: He chose human life as His dwelling place. His presence and His purpose put us on holy ground.

It is Christ who is the visible expression of the invisible God.

W. PHILLIP
KELLER

✷

What does that mean? *God is with us. . . .* In the deadlines, in the splendor, in the singing of a bird, . . . in the plumbing repair, in a friend's phone call. He is there in it all.

Week 4

SUZANNE DALE EZELL
Living Simply in God's Abundance

The pedigree of honey
Does not concern the bee;
A clover, any time, to him
Is aristocracy.

EMILY
DICKINSON
(1830–1886)

The Somewhere Woman

✹

Draw near to God and He will draw near to you.

James 4:8

The somewhere woman is a happy woman! She knows exactly where she's going and how she's going to get there.

She has been given a map—the law of the Lord, the Bible. She thinks about and studies and meditates on this map until she is thoroughly familiar with the road she is to take. . . .

I get a picture of an intent traveler, poring over a map, trying to choose the best road, seeking to avoid needless hazards. . . . She will be able to see the hazards, the rest areas, and the bad corners. She will have instructions about her speed and behavior as she drives her car along. . . .

It is as silly for a Christian to set out upon the journey of life without the Bible to guide them as it is for a traveler to set off without a map.

JILL BRISCOE
Quiet Times with God

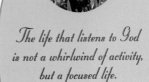

The life that listens to God is not a whirlwind of activity, but a focused life.

WAYNE
JACOBSEN

Plantings of the Heart

So we, being many, are one body in Christ,
and individually members of one another.

Romans 12:5

The mysteries of God surround me in the handkerchief-size garden which seemed advisable after the harsh winter. The zucchini vine covers itself with trumpet-shaped blooms, dumps its vegetables and wanders on—probably into my neighbor's yard. I never realized how much one squash vine could yield. I knew what, however, because I knew what kind of seed I had sown.

The same is true of deeds we do. We can measure neither the rate of growth nor the yield. Selfishly, I should like to be able to gather in an armload of proofs of my planting, but my job is to continue sowing. I may never see maturity, but I have God's reassurance that it will occur. . . .

Dr. Albert Schweitzer wrote: "I do not know what your destiny will be, but of one thing I am certain—the only ones among you who will be truly happy are those who have sought and found how to serve." These are the plantings, yes; and God tells us what the harvest will be: nothing less than everlasting life.

JUNE MASTERS BACHER
Quiet Moments for Women

Think of God's Love

***

Beloved, if God so loved us, we also ought to love one another.

1 John 4:11

The only crown Jesus ever wore on earth was a crown of thorns.

What does that crown tell us about the love of God the Father? Much every way. For one thing, it tells us that His love is not a sentimental thing, for it was strong enough to hurt His own Son. He could have rescued Him with "legions of angels." He did not do so.

What does the crown of thorns tell us about the love of God the Son? It tells us that it was strong enough to deny itself, strong enough to suffer. He could have evaded the crown and the Cross. If He had taken Satan up on his offers in the wilderness He would have evaded both. He did not do so. He had set His face like a flint, and moved with flint–like resolution down that course, with all its humiliations, interruptions, demands, disappointments, and deprivations. . . . He went straight to Jerusalem, and He went filled with joy and gratitude and love.

The Cross of Jesus is the supreme evidence of the love of God.

OSWALD
CHAMBERS

*

ELISABETH ELLIOT
The Path of Loneliness

Cream-colored bank
roses bloomed along
Old Church Lane,
forming billowy clouds
over the emerald grass.

JAN KARON

*These High
Green Hills*

God—the Source of All Security

*Walk worthy of the calling with which you were
called, with all lowliness and gentleness.*

Ephesians 4:1

Parents who teach their children that they are precious children of God lead their youngsters straight to the source of all security. However, many parents can't teach this to their children. They've either lost this belief about themselves, or their own parents never gave them this priceless message. Instead, children flounder in a sea of insecurity, clinging to various rafts as lifesavers: looks, intelligence, family background, money, athletic prowess, or whatever it is that gives a measure of approval or satisfaction.

I spent many of my teen and young adult years clinging to various life rafts: I learned not to walk into a lunchroom without a friend; not to speak up in class; not to sing above a murmur at church; not to buy clothes except certain "in" styles.

What I've learned since is that God wants us to be ourselves, to be secure in our own skins. He gave us personalities and gifts, and He wants us to glisten radiantly. When we are free of our false inhibitions, we are free to love each other and to live full and happy lives.

*God's heart is enlarged
to take us in.*

RICHARD J.
FOSTER

LESLIE WILLIAMS
Seduction of the Lesser Gods

Notes

Today I held God in my hands
Within a bright bouquet
Of freshly–gathered flowers
I picked and gave away.

JUNE   MASTERS   BACHER
Quiet Moments for Women

Bone-Deep Honesty

✳

Be steadfast, immovable, always abounding in the work of the Lord.
1 Corinthians 15:58

What is God looking for? He is looking for men and women whose hearts are completely His—*completely*. God is not looking for magnificent specimens of humanity. He's looking for deeply spiritual, genuinely humble, honest–to–the–core servants who have integrity.

Listen to some of the synonyms for this Hebrew word *thamam*, translated "integrity": "complete, whole, innocent, having simplicity of life, wholesome, sound, unimpaired." Isn't that beautiful? Integrity is what you are when nobody's looking. It means being bone–deep honest.

Today, we live in a world that says, in many ways, "If you just make a good impression, that's all that matters." But you will never be a man or woman of God if that's your philosophy. Never. You cannot fake it with the Almighty. He is not impressed with externals. He always focuses on the inward qualities . . . those things that take time and discipline to cultivate.

My worth to God in public is what I am in private.

OSWALD
CHAMBERS

✳

CHARLES R. SWINDOLL
David: A Man of Passion and Destiny

*Nothing could surpass
a tomato picked and
eaten, still sun-hot, on
a drowsy summer's
afternoon.*

MARJORIE
HOLMES
Lord Let Me Love

Sloshing Annoyances

✳

*My lips shall greatly rejoice when I sing to You,
and my soul, which You have redeemed.*

Psalm 71:23

It was a great day when my father brought home the hand-crank cream separator. . . . I insisted on standing on a stool to ladle the milk into the enormous milk container. . . .

Daddy brought the still-warm jersey milk from the barn and I had him set the galvanized pails near the new contraption and hurriedly began. It was such fun that I failed to see the "Fill it to here" line. In my enthusiasm, I filled the container to the top. The result was disastrous. The first turn of the crank sent milk splashing all over my checked apron, into Daddy's face, onto Mama's freshly done-up gingham curtains, and onto her spotless linoleum. . . .

Many times I have thought of what happens to my day when I allow it to be filled beyond the danger point with annoyances, petty thinking, and unworthy thoughts. Sooner or later they're going to slosh out all over those around me. . . . So I take a day gone ragged with care and let the sunshine and the bird song take over. How refreshing! . . . And all it takes is a little turn of the spigot of the mind.

*May I engage in nothing
in which I cannot implore
thy blessing, and in which
I cannot invite thy inspection.*

PURITAN
PRAYER

✳

Week 5

JUNE MASTERS BACHER
The Quiet Heart

I often think flowers are the angel's alphabet whereby they write on hills and fields mysterious and beautiful lessons for us to feel and learn.

LOUISA MAY
ALCOTT

Taking Little Steps

✳

Be tenderhearted, be courteous . . . that you may inherit a blessing.

1 Peter 3:9

God delights when He sees those whom He created in His own image display little bits of that image in their lives.

When we're creative, He enjoys the labors of our hands. When we give of ourselves and our possessions, He applauds. When we're merciful, extending grace and forgiveness to those who have hurt us, He cheers. And when we do right, standing up for His will and way, He absolutely loves it. . . .

He beholds us, He watches us, and He encourages us to take little steps as we follow the example of His Son.

And it brings Him great joy. Joy that shines right back on us.

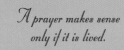

A prayer makes sense only if it is lived.

ANTHONY BLOOM

✳

PETER WALLACE
What the Psalmist Is Saying to You Today

There Be Dragons Here

*He who searches the hearts knows what the mind of the
Spirit is, because He makes intercession for the saints.*

Romans 8:27

In ancient times, when men and women held to the
certainty that the world was flat, maps of the seas often
depicted the end of the earth as a huge cliff. There, a
cataract of ocean waters plunged forever into a bottomless
chasm, and near the edge of the waterfall, the charts bore the
warning: *There Be Dragons Here.*

Sometimes I think I should write that warning, or a modified
version of it, on the face page of my Bible.

The reality of the dragons, of the struggles we must face if we
leave the protection of our safe places, in no way contradicts the
promises of a loving God. But we need to be very clear about
the promises. God does not promise happiness; God offers
growth. The Lord holds out challenge, not comfort; fortitude, not
escape.

PENELOPE J. STOKES
Faith: The Substance of Things Unseen

God Blesses a Thankful Heart

✳

*Keep yourselves in the love of God, looking for the mercy
of our Lord Jesus Christ unto eternal life.*

Jude 20

As we rode along, I forgot my awe of Papa and we talked about the time we came to Saskatchewan and lived in the chicken house. "Do you remember the chicken house, Papa?"

Papa's laughter rolled over the prairie as we remembered together. . . .

Even now I could hear the sound of that first night—wind over the prairie, mice scampering about, flies buzzing on the sticky fly paper, and the lonely howl of a coyote.

"But Papa," I ventured now, "that farmer said his barn was full."

"Ja, but the wife had the key."

I had watched, bewildered, as the farmer's wife carefully counted the eggs and offered skimmed milk, a bowl of flour, and a bowl of sugar. "They had so much, Papa, and gave so little—and you and Mama have so little and give so much."

"I know, Margaret, I know. It is all such a mystery," Papa said solemnly. "The poor heard Jesus gladly, and the poor give cheerfully. But always remember Margaret, it is the spirit of giving that God blesses—and a thankful heart, like Mama says."

*Love is the doorway through
which the human soul passes
from selfishness to service.*

ANONYMOUS

MARGARET JENSEN
Papa's Place

When the God of the
universe offers to share
with each of us all He is,
that's a good deal!

GLORIA GAITHER
Because He Lives

Christmas in the Summertime

✳

*What does the LORD require of you but to do justly,
to love mercy, and to walk humbly with your God?*

Micah 6 : 8

Some people live with a low-grade anxiety tugging at their spirit all day long. They go to sleep with it, wake up with it, carry it around at home, in town, to church, and with friends. Here's a remedy: Take the present moment and find something to laugh at. People who laugh, last.

Another happily-ever-after idea is to celebrate Christmas all year round. Doesn't everyone wish the contagious joy of the holidays would seep into summer? You'll find ways to make it happen if you pay attention to people. See what they're good at and give them a compliment. Pick up on their personal burdens and offer to carry one for a while. Keep smiles ready to hand out. Buy somebody a cup of coffee. . . .

It is never too late to spend time on the important things. It is never too late to do what makes you happy. There is always time to look around and see something beautiful.

Every bit of love upon God's earth has God at the other end of it.

MARK GUY
PEARSE

BARBARA JOHNSON
Joy Breaks

Notes

We are not idle during summer,
but we keep busy with holy play.

HARRIET CROSBY

Quiet in God

✴

Create in me a clean heart, O God,
and renew a steadfast spirit within me.

Psalm 51:10

*P*rayer is worship. Our praying should be full of
adoration, affection, and fondness for God.
It is one of the best ways in the world to
love him.

Prayer is petition. We can ask for anything even
the most difficult things—and know that God hears
us. . . .

Prayer is asking for understanding. It is the
means by which we comprehend what God is
saying to us in his Word. . . .

Prayer is all these things but it is more: *it is the*
means by which we fit in. It is the way God aligns us
with him and enables us to collaborate with him in
complete union and oneness. Seen in that way, prayer is
more like *listening* than anything else—being quiet in God's
presence, waiting on God until we know what to do.

Anything big enough to
occupy our minds is big enough
to hang a prayer on.

GEORGE
MACDONALD

✴

DAVID ROPER
Elijah: A Man Like Us

Oh, sacrament of summer days,
Oh, last communion in the haze,
    Permit a child to join,

Thy sacred emblems to partake,
Thy consecrated bread to break,
    Taste thine immortal wine!

EMILY DICKINSON

O Lord of the oceans,
My little bark sails on
a restless sea,
Grant that Jesus may
sit at the helm
And steer me safely.

PURITAN PRAYER

God Sets the Boundaries

✷

I have taught you in the way of wisdom; I have led you in right paths.

PROVERBS 4:11

I love the sea. I love the beauty and the terror of it. I love the certainty and the uncertainty of it, its amazing power and its sweet gentleness. It reminds me never to limit myself to believing merely in the possible, and most of all, never to limit God to what seems "possible." It reminds me that a God who can be explained by my mind is no God at all, but an idol constructed by my own hands or, worse, a house pet led on a leash. I must stand beside the ocean often so I will not forget that I am not the cre-ator of the universe and that I must never create God in my image. His ways are immensely higher than my ways.

God's promises are always broader than our prayers.

FRANCES HAVERGAL

✷

When I worry about relationships that seem to come and go, I must let the tide teach me that there is an ebb and flow to everything, and that the tide that goes out will, in due time, return if I just trust the God who sets the boundaries and is the measure of all things.

GLORIA GAITHER
Because He Lives

Bees and butterflies create waves of soft, silent colors in my garden. . . . They flock around the lantana . . . congregating as if at a tea party.

LAURA MARTIN

Nesting in God's Love

✳

*He shall cover you with His feathers, and
under His wings you shall take refuge.*

Psalm 91:4

A mother bird is a fascinating creature, capable of warm, careful concern, on the one hand, and fierce protective defense of her children, on the other.

And in that illustration you can catch a glimpse of God's care for you. God covers you with His wings so you are warm and protected from the elements. You are able to grow as you should. All your needs are provided. And you can nest in His love.

And when you do venture out from the nest, trying your own wings, you can always fly back to Him and find refuge and safety under His wings.

As you grow, He provides the defense and strength you need as you face the world. Wherever you go, you can take His truth with you as a shield from enemy attack and from emotional harm.

*People who move the world
are the ones who do not let
the world move them.*

ANONYMOUS

PETER WALLACE
What the Psalmist Is Saying to You Today

Life is for Loving

✳

Come to Me, all you who labor . . . and I will give you rest.
Matthew 11:28

Despite our ever-increasing affluence, despite our shorter workweeks, . . . despite our more advanced technology, despite our improved social benefits, men and women are today probably more restless, more uneasy, and more discontented than ever before. Life for most seems to be a strained state of apprehension and tension. They seem to be caught up in an ever-accelerating stream of events over which they have little or no control. They are swept along on the swirling current of circumstances which leaves them dazed and bewildered. . . .

This is a most wearing way to live. It erodes away the zest for living. It robs men and women of quiet serenity. It denies them the great calm assurance of knowing where they are going.

But once we have come into contact with Christ and recognize the great honors and privileges bestowed on us in being God's children this all changes. . . . We discover that life is for learning, learning how better to love God and love our fellow men and love all that is worthwhile in the world.

W. PHILLIP KELLER
Taming Tension

Stargazing

✳

The heavens declare the glory of God;
and the firmament shows His handiwork.

P s a l m   1 9 : 1

*I*s there any better time of year than summer to
go stargazing? Warm nights, crickets chirping,
honeysuckle in the breeze, and a big black sky
full of stars. You can lie on a blanket on the lawn
or in the sand at the ocean or under your sleep-
ing bag on a backpacking trip in the mountains.
And to think that on any given night you and I
are seeing the same stars—the Big Dipper,
Orion, the Pleiades. I can't imagine that anyone
could spend a night under the stars and not
consider that there might be someone bigger than
us, who somehow tossed these diamonds about the
heavens. I like what the philosopher Immanuel Kant
had to say. "Two things fill the mind with ever new and
increasing wonder and awe—the starry heavens above me and
the moral law within me." . . .

When was the last time you gazed into the night sky? The
psalmist states that the heavens declare God's glory.

God is in this place,
even when you are
unaware of it.

PENELOPE
J. STOKES

✳

BERNIE SHEAHAN
Soul Searching

Herbs should certainly
form part of any
vegetable garden,
be it a humble patch
or a grand enclosure.

MALCOLM
HILLIER

The Herb Garden

Glad Is Great

✳

Celebrate . . . with gladness, both with thanksgiving and singing.

NEHEMIAH 12:27

In the bottom drawer of the kitchen cabinet is a handy box of clear polyethylene, better known as GLAD Cling Wrap. Good stuff, this. The box proudly proclaims all the benefits of being GLAD:

GLAD Is Easy to Handle. I couldn't agree more. Give me a glad person to work with, any day. Not overly sensitive, not demanding, just glad to be alive and easy to get along with.

GLAD Keeps Things Fresh. Nothing like a new perspective to make life interesting. People who are glad are fun to be around—refreshing, in fact. . . .

GLAD Is Great for All Uses. Don't you love those flexible folks who are glad to be useful and can do anything you ask without complaining? . . .

You see, glad is a handy thing to be in God's kingdom. Those who are glad are able to rejoice and shout for joy with an *exclamation point!* As a writer who loves that form of punctuation, I get excited when it shows up in Scripture. We're talking big happy here! Be ye glad.

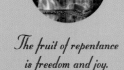

The fruit of repentance is freedom and joy.

HARRIET CROSBY

✳

LIZ CURTIS HIGGS
Reflecting His Image

Notes

*Bend your head in the dewy freshness of every morning,
ere you go forth to meet the day's duties and perils,
and wait for the benediction of Christ
as He lays His hands upon you.*

J .   R .   M I L L E R

Attached to the Fixed Point

✳

The statutes of the LORD are right, rejoicing the heart;
the commandment of the LORD is pure, enlightening the eyes.

Psalm 19:8

My life always seems off-balance. I've thought sometimes of the Foucault pendulum, swinging first to one side, returning to center only to swing far to the other side. Even with heroic effort I can't remain in that perfectly aligned centered spot. And yet ironically there is a certain balance achieved by swinging first one way and then allowing oneself to be tugged back. I often feel off-balance, and yet in my imbalance there is (I'm beginning to believe) a kind of balance. The secret to the pendulum's ability to maintain an equilibrium . . . is the cable attached to a fixed point at the top of the dome.

Tears are God's way of helping us descend with the mind into the heart.

RICHARD
FOSTER

Like the pendulum attached by a cable to the ceiling, we are free, when in touch with our fixed point, to swing back and forth, to err and correct our swing, to remain off-balance while essentially being in balance. There is stability and dynamism in this image. We swing in response to events and people in our days, but we are secure in a central relationship with Jesus Christ.

SARA WENGER SHANK
Coming Home

In summer we lived
much as the birds did,
on our fruit and bread
and milk;
the sun was our fire,
the sky our roof.

LOUISA MAY
ALCOTT

The Best Part Is Getting There

✳

Your ears shall hear a voice behind you,
saying, "This is the way; walk in it."

Isaiah 30:21

We cannot stay in spiritual suburbia if we want to see the miracle in the desert.

PENELOPE J.
STOKES

✳

For me, the best part of a trip is always getting there. When I was little, I would clamor to sit in the front seat of the car. I loved sitting next to my dad so I could spread out a map on my lap and help him navigate. The lines on the map would turn from thick red to thin black when the road got narrow. We'd pass farms and villages, and I would always mark off on the map each milestone.

I've always enjoyed maps. I feel good when I have a decent idea of where I'm going and how to get there. A map allows me to mark off progress, to help me see how much farther I have to go.

That's why I enjoy my walk with Jesus. His Word is just like a map. Pick a verse, any verse, and you're on your way. God orders your steps. He points to the narrow road rather than the broad one. He says, "I am the way" and you certainly can't get lost when you tailgate the Lord.

Week 7

JONI EARECKSON TADA
Diamonds in the Dust

Thy Word is full of promises,
flowers of sweet fragrance
fruit of refreshing flavor
when culled by faith.
PURITAN PRAYER

A New Beginning

✳

I will . . . bind up the broken and strengthen what was sick.

Ezekiel 34:16

I was at Land's End, the most southerly tip of England. A plaque on a house there reads "This is the last house in England and the first." I thought about that for a while. Of course, it all depends on which direction you are facing. If you stand with your back to Cornwall and your face to France, indeed it is the last house in England. But if you stand with your back to the ocean and your face toward England, it is just the beginning. . . .

There have been times when I have fallen exhausted at the feet of Christ with nowhere left to turn—but I have found it to be a beginning and not the end. I may have been at the end of my ideas and my self-confidence, the end of my ability, but in truth I was at a new beginning. The beginning of listening to God, being directed by him, finding rest in him.

SHEILA WALSH
Gifts for Your Soul

God's will is what He sovereignly purposes and plans, and as such it cannot be improved.

J. OSWALD SANDERS

✳

Life-Giving Power

Your word is a lamp to my feet and a light to my path.

Psalm 119:105

At the most difficult times in my life—the loss of a baby, the forced removal from a church, the execution of a friend, the robbery of our home—God's Word has sustained me. There have been times when I have only been capable of reading a few verses at a time, yet the supernatural life-giving power of the Word of God has not only helped me maintain my emotional and mental balance, it has given me strength to go on, even if only one day at a time.

There is strength . . .

There is peace . . .

There is hope . . .

There is power . . .

Read the Word.

ANNE GRAHAM LOTZ
The Vision of His Glory

Deep Roots Endure

✳

*May the Lord make you increase and abound
in love to one another and to all.*

1 T h e s s a l o n i a n s 3 : 1 2

O ne warm summer day I went in search of a special Ollala bush that I had marked carefully on one of my hikes. It stood all alone on a steep, stony slope far removed from any other bushes of its kind. It was laden with beautiful berries of unusual size. . . .

As I picked my share I marveled at such bounty coming from an uncultivated, untended tree in such an unlikely spot. Here the soil was thin, stony, riddled with rocks, and baked by the relentless sun. The seasonal winds whipped the bush back and forth without mercy, lashing its limbs with every savage blow. . . .

With deep-watered roots we never lack—no matter how hot and dry the summer.

WAYNE
JACOBSEN

In spite of all the adversities of its environment, all the abuse of rough weather, all the stresses of its stem and tough location, the Olalla bush flowered and fruited in this spot with joyous abandon because of its deep roots.

It was a vivid, living demonstration of that ancient adage— *"Just bloom where you are planted!"* It sounds so simple. Sometimes it has an almost romantic touch to it. [But] to do so takes deep roots!

W. PHILLIP KELLER
Songs of My Soul

*Pink and fuchsia
climbers massed
themselves on trellises,
and in one yard,
a vast stand of old
shrub roses cast
their rich, heavy
perfume on the air.*

JAN KARON

*These High
Green Hills*

Time for Beauty

✳

You have put gladness in my heart.

P s a l m   4 : 7

Lord, let me take time for beauty.
Time for a jug of flowers on the table, or a plant if flowers aren't in bloom. . . . Don't let me settle for the dingy, the shabby, the ugly—either with myself or with my house, just because I'm too lazy to make the effort. . . .

You've made the world so beautiful, Lord, let me take time to see it. Even as I'm rushing to the market or driving children to their destinations, let me be aware of it: the glory of hills and woods and shining water. The colors of traffic lights and yellow buses, of fruit stands and lumberyards, of girls wearing bright scarves that dance in the breeze.

Let me take time for the beauty in my own backyard, Lord.

Let me lift my eyes from the dishes to rejoice in the sunshine spilling through the trees. In the squirrels darting jaunty-plumed along the bleached boards of the fence. In the raindrops strung out on the clothesline like a string of crystal beads.

*The fruit of holy obedience
is the simplicity of the
children of God.*

THOMAS
KELLY

✳

MARJORIE HOLMES
Lord Let Me Love

Notes

Plough deep in me, great Lord, . . .
That my being may be a tilled field,
The roots of grace spreading far and wide,
Until thou alone art seen in me,
Thy beauty golden like summer harvest.

PURITAN PRAYER

What Jesus Stood For

✳

*I applied my heart to know, to search and
seek out wisdom and the reason for things.*

ECCLESIASTES 7:25

*I*n Jesus' time, the Pharisees had clearly defined what
they stood *against*. Over generations, using the
basic laws of the Ten Commandments and the
teachings of Moses, they had developed a vast
legalistic structure—to the point that they argued
whether it was lawful to eat an egg laid on the
Sabbath.

They were against travel on the Sabbath. They
were against impurity. They were against women
in the inner court of the temple. Most of all in
their self-righteousness, they were against the
people who failed to follow their religious rules.

Jesus? In the two great commandments—love God,
love your neighbor—he stated not what he stood against
but what he stood *for*. For healing, even on a Sabbath. For
forgiveness, not of sin but of the sinner. For reaching out to
those in need. For love.

And when he died on the cross, Jesus stood for us all.

SIGMUND BROUWER
The Carpenter's Cloth

*Religion is simple.
Spiritual life is difficult.*

PENELOPE J.
STOKES

✳

The garden at teatime is
still my favorite place
on earth to savor the
moment and deepen my
affection for life.

ALEXANDRA
STODDARD

A Tiny Seed of Faith

✳

If you have faith as a mustard seed, . . .
nothing will be impossible for you.

Matthew 17:20

My whole garden started with my planting tiny catnip seeds. Eventually, one small seed grew into a bush three-and-a-half feet high and about three feet in diameter. And all the cats in the neighborhood now come to nest in its branches.

The mustard seed is one of the smallest seeds in the world. It takes very little faith to grow big miracles. But sometimes I find having even the smallest amount of faith the most difficult thing in the world—especially when times are hard. I recently experienced a series of painful losses. I found that simply having faith the size of a mustard seed became miracle enough, never mind moving mountains.

Prayer is the path where there is none.

NOAH BENSHEA

✳

Jesus gave this teaching to a church experiencing severe trials and persecution. It is a teaching for the painful times in our lives, one that tells us to cultivate faith the size of a very tiny seed and let it grow in the ground of our own pain. Such faith sown in pain is a miracle great enough to move mountains.

Week 8

HARRIET CROSBY
A Well-Watered Garden

*The summer market is
alive with color, and no
one can scoop up enough
fruit to make up for
winter's dearth.*

GEORGEANNE
BRENNAN

The Potager

Listening for God's Voice

The LORD your God himself crosses over before you. . . .
He will be with you, He will not leave you nor forsake you.

D e u t e r o n o m y   3 1 : 3

"Stay within hearing distance," my father cautioned the day I went with him to haul firewood. But the dogwood was in full bloom, each tree a bit more beautiful—and a little farther away. I wandered on and on, forgetting Daddy's warning. Soon I was lost. . . .

I panicked and began to scream hearing only a mocking echo that seemed to come from the four directions.

Wait for God. Wait on God. Wait with God.

A N N E
O R T L U N D

At last my voice and legs gave way to exhaustion. I sat down on the mossy bank of a little stream and prepared to die. But it was in that quiet moment that I heard a dearly familiar voice. Daddy was calling my name!

What had happened? I was able to hear only when I stopped my screaming. Then, as I listened, calmly and reassuringly, my father guided me to him.

How good to know that our heavenly Father is always within "hearing distance" even when we forget and wander away. No matter how far we wander, . . . God can and *will* lead us home if we will but listen for His voice.

JUNE MASTERS BACHER
The Quiet Heart

Knowing God's Will

The plans of the diligent lead surely to plenty.

P r o v e r b s   21:5

Our steps, Solomon assures us, are "directed by the Lord." But what does that mean? It means that

if we concern ourselves with his will
if we obey each day his directions
if we heed each day his warnings
if we walk by faith
if we step out daily along the path of obedience as best we
    understand it

we will find that God takes responsibility for our decisions and actions. He will set us about his intended purpose. He will get us to the right person in the right place at the right time.

God's will is easy to find—if we want it. Really, the only people who miss his will are those who have no use for it. The months and years may show us that we've taken a strange, roundabout way, but if our hearts are right, our feet will never go astray. We will know what God wants us to do.

D A V I D   R O P E R
Elijah: A Man Like Us

Freedom from Anxiety

✻

Do not store up for yourselves treasure on earth. . . .

MATTHEW 6:19

The young Francis of Assisi, believing that he was
to be espoused to "Lady Poverty," stripped off
his clothes and threw them on the ground.

"From now on," he said to the crowd in front of
the bishop's palace, "I can advance naked before
the Lord, saying in truth no longer: my father,
Peter Bernardone, but: our Father which art in
heaven!"

The bishop's gardener gave him a little coat,
full of holes, on which he drew a chalk cross.
Then he set out through the woods, singing the
Lord's praises at the top of his lungs.

Not all Christians are bound to strip themselves
naked and go singing into the woods, but all Christians
are bound to have the same attitude of utter freedom from
anxiety that enabled Saint Francis to sing.

The heart that is reluctant to receive joyfully all of God's good
gifts is also reluctant to part with any of them.

ELISABETH ELLIOT
Discipline: The Glad Surrender

*Love stretches your heart and
makes you big inside.*

MARGARET
WALKER

✻

"Garden's up!" First,
the round pushy radish
leaves; then the tiny
points of onions,
followed by a delicate
dance of lettuce shifting
through.

MARJORIE HOLMES

Lord Let Me Love

"Soft" Times for the Soul

✳

I command you today to love the LORD your God, to walk in His ways, and to keep His commandments.

DEUTERONOMY 30:16

*I*f you've seen pictures of Ireland, you know how green it is over there. I found out why when I visited a few years back. It rains almost every day, even in the summer. But it's rarely torrential or violent. Often the rain comes down in gentle showers or mist, what the Irish call "soft" days.

Rain does soften the day and quiet the world. Sun is loud—it just calls for shouting. Notice the birds; even they are quiet when the rain falls.

Now, I'm one who enjoys a boisterous summer day, with children laughing and birds chirping and even cars honking. But it's nice to have a rainy day every once in a while. It's a good time to get quiet, to be reflective, and to slow down just a bit.

What happens to you on a rainy day? Do you see it as an intrusion . . . ? Or do you accept a rainy day as God's way of getting you to slow down? Rain waters the grass and makes the flowers grow. Can it give some refreshment to your spirit?

Obedience is the soul of knowledge.

GEORGE MACDONALD

✳

BERNIE SHEAHAN
Soul Searching

Notes

For blue of stream, for blue of sky;
For pleasant shade of branches high;
For fragrant air and cooling breeze;
For beauty of the blowing trees—
Father in Heaven, we thank Thee!

RALPH WALDO EMERSON
(1 8 0 2 - 1 8 8 2)

Trust God and Be Quiet

✳

To Him who is able to keep you from
stumbling . . . be glory and majesty.

J u d e   2 4 ,   2 5

rue waiting on God is not "doing nothing."
Psalm 37 lists the principal elements of this
hidden activity, a perfect formula for peace of
mind . . . :

Trust in the Lord and do good.

Dwell in the land (make your home, settle
down, be at peace where God puts you).

Delight in the Lord (make the Lord your only
joy) and He will give you what your heart
desires. . . .

Our thoughts are the fabric
with which we weave our
character and destiny.

RANDY
ALCORN

Trust in Him and He will act. Be *quiet* before the
Lord.

Wait patiently for Him, not worrying about others.

Waiting patiently is almost impossible unless we also
are learning at the same time to find joy in the Lord, commit
everything to Him, trust Him, and be quiet.

ELISABETH ELLIOT
The Path of Loneliness

I have always assigned a
certain intelligence to
sunflowers. Their great,
golden-bonneted heads
follow their Master
from horizon to horizon.
Would that we did the
same for Him.

**JUNE MASTERS
BACHER**

The Quiet Heart

A Heavenly Catalog

Not one [sparrow] falls to the ground apart from your Father's will.

MATTHEW 10:29

I love ordering things from clothes catalogs. The order forms . . . are like crossword puzzles—but with all the answers provided. I feel really great, clever, and all that because I can fill them in!

The order is mailed and forgotten in the rush of more immediate things. Then *bang,* right in the middle of some activity totally unrelated to my catalog order, the parcel is delivered!

How like God. The specifics of my order are carefully tabulated and delivered in his time and with eternal efficiency. The answers are sent to prayers I prayed months, even years, ago—long after I have forgotten my requests. Sometimes it no longer really matters to me if the parcel even arrives! But my words are not allowed to fall to the ground. Angels catch them and register the demand. How good of God.

Prayer is always the preface to blessing.

CHARLES
SPURGEON

JILL
BRISCOE
Quiet Times with God

Week 9

*Flowers are angels
rooted in soil.*
ALEXANDRA
STODDARD

Moments Wrapped in Ribbon

✳

Oh, satisfy us early with Your mercy,
that we may rejoice and be glad all our days!

Psalm 90:14

*E*very day is a most amazing day, if we have eyes to see it, ears to hear it, active senses to wrap around and enter into it. The world is studded and strewn with wonders—acts of unexpected kindness, moments of true companionship, music to touch a deep spot of pain. . . . Most of us hardly notice, rushing pell-mell toward who knows where. We haven't cultivated worship in tiny moments spread throughout the day; we leave it rather for sanctimonious Sunday mornings. But worship is a daily, moment-by-moment exercise. It is like breathing and knowing with each breath that life is a gift; each moment is wrapped with a ribbon of God's presence. . . .

What more than all else energizes our desire to celebrate? . . .

It all comes of a love affair with the Creator. It comes of a love that has so profoundly awakened us to newness of life that we ache to respond, we long to celebrate.

Thou hast died for me; may I live to thee, in every moment of my time . . . in every pulse of my heart.

PURITAN
PRAYER

✳

SARA WENGER SHANK
Coming Home

The Heart's True Home

✳

We have blessed you from the house of the Lord.

Psalm 118:26

As I was agonizing about whether to buy my house, a well-meaning friend said to me, "Look. A house is just shelter. Nothing more. That's how you have to think about it." Others have since espoused this real estate philosophy. I find such philosophy sadly lacking. . . . Buying a home is as much a matter of the heart as the head.

My home is a living, creative work in process. Homemaking, which in my view includes gardening, is a creative effort. It is much more than dusting once a week, cleaning the bathroom, or cooking dinner. Nor is it weeding, watering, or fertilizing. Homemaking is the art of making a home out of a house and a garden out of a wasteland. . . . Homemaking is a form of self-expression. Homemaking and gardening creatively express those unique dreams, emotions, and memories each of us has inside us about home. And about Christ, our heart's true home.

HARRIET CROSBY
A Place Called Home

Love Works Hard

✳

Love bears all things, believes all things,
hopes all things, endures all things.

1 Corinthians 13:7

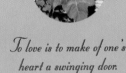

Love isn't just a kind of soft feeling, a thrill of honeysuckle fragrance while being kissed on a June night. Love isn't just happiness in ideal situations with everything going according to daydreams of family life or married life or parent–child closeness and confidences. Love has work to do! . . .

To love is to make of one's heart a swinging door.

HOWARD
THURMAN

✳

Husband–wife love, wife–husband love, and parent–child love—in times of weakness and failure, when forgiveness must be asked for and given, in times when suspicions have been right— love goes on. A child needs to grow up knowing that love never faileth, that not only will Dad and Mom stay together in spite of each of their weaknesses as well as strengths, but that the door will always be open, the "candle in the window" will never go out. . . . Love keeps that door open, the light waiting, and dinner in the oven—for years.

EDITH SCHAEFFER
What Is a Family?

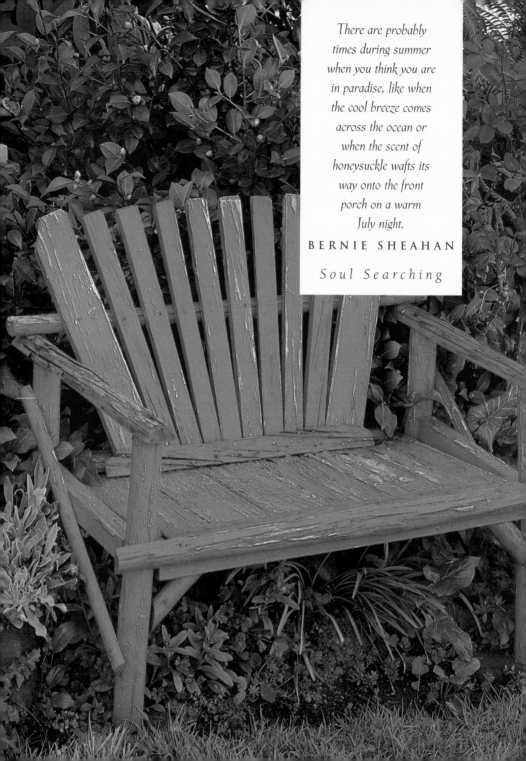

There are probably
times during summer
when you think you are
in paradise, like when
the cool breeze comes
across the ocean or
when the scent of
honeysuckle wafts its
way onto the front
porch on a warm
July night.

BERNIE SHEAHAN

Soul Searching

Faith and Power Go Hand in Hand

Always pursue what is good both for yourselves and for all.

1 Thessalonians 5:15

There is no question that life is difficult and uncertain. In the blink of an eye, life can come crashing down around us like a rain of brimstone. Whether these crises come at a bedside, a graveside, a roadside, or in a marriage, a relationship, an office, or a church setting, the results can leave us devastated—weak-kneed and shattered.

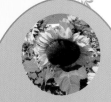

God is with us. It is enough.

PENELOPE J. STOKES

These are the moments faith is made of. The Bible supports this, and I have seen it time after time in my own life and in others'. The more we need faith, the more faith we are given. The more we completely trust God, the deeper that trust grows.

Faith and power are gifts that go hand in hand, and they come from the source of all power, the Holy Spirit. . . . God's gifts of faith and power are always adequate, no matter how desperate our situation has become.

SUZANNE DALE EZELL
Living Simply in God's Abundance

Notes

Speak gently—'tis a little thing
Dropp'd in the heart's deep well;
The good, the joy which it may bring,
Eternity shall tell.

ANONYMOUS

The Task of a Lifetime

✴

*Though He was a Son, yet He learned
obedience by the things which He suffered.*

Hebrews 5:8

*I*f you want to be a person with a large vision,
you must cultivate the habit of doing the little
things well. That's when God puts iron in
your bones! . . . The test of my calling is not how
well I do before the public on Sunday; it's how
carefully I cover the bases Monday through
Saturday when there's nobody to check up on me,
when nobody is looking. . . .

When God develops character, He works on it
throughout a lifetime. He's never in a hurry.

It is in the schoolroom of solitude and obscurity
that we learn to become men and women of God. It is
from the schoolmasters of monotony and reality that we
learn to "king it." That's how we become—like David—
men and women after God's own heart.

CHARLES SWINDOLL
David: Man of Passion and Destiny

*We are not meant to live
merely by what is natural.
We need to learn to live
by the supernatural.*

ELISABETH
ELLIOT

✴

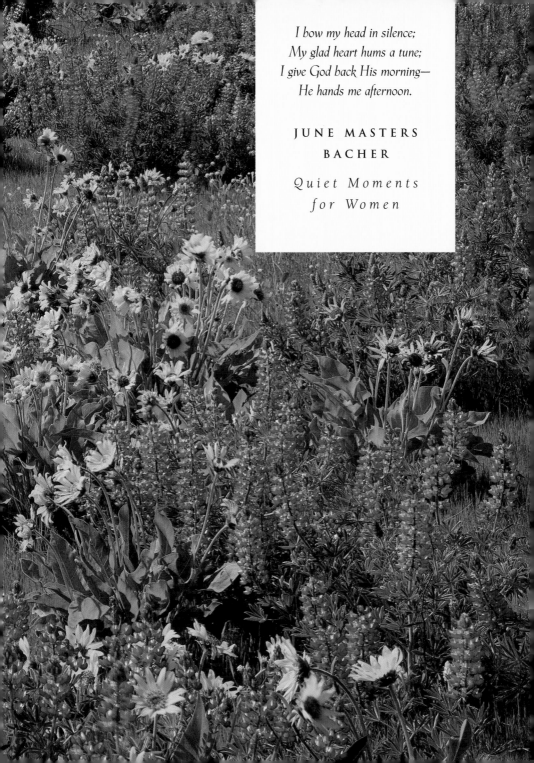

I bow my head in silence;
My glad heart hums a tune;
I give God back His morning—
He hands me afternoon.

JUNE MASTERS
BACHER

*Quiet Moments
for Women*

I love the sound of water
lapping at the bottom of a
fishing boat after dark and
of paddles dipping deep
and strong to bring weary
children back to the
lakeshore.

GLORIA GAITHER

Because He Lives

summer - week ten

God's Teaching Tools

✳

And you shall know the truth, and the truth shall make you free.

John 8:32

God shows us the direction to heaven by pointing the fingers of the tallest mountain peaks upward where dark vagabond clouds linger to teach of a silver lining.

- God reveals His caring for the creatures He created by watering the fields in softly singing rains.

- God demonstrates how He can cast away our cares by planting fields of wildflowers, so bright of spirit, so gloriously robed, and taking no thought of tomorrow's changes.

- God illustrates His own desire to pull our wandering feet home to His kingdom by magnetizing the hearts of His lesser beings so that they are drawn to the nest, the burrow, and the glen.

- God whispers of foreverness in the drop of the sun—its golden hush reflected in the wings of birds in homeward flight—the brief twilight, and then the resurrection of a new day.

The great need is not to do things, but to believe things.

OSWALD
CHAMBERS

✳

Week 10

JUNE MASTERS BACHER
The Quiet Heart

The robins stand as
thick today
As flakes of snow
stood yesterday,
On fence and roof
and twig.

EMILY
DICKINSON

(1830–1886)

Living a Creative Life

✳

We speak, not as pleasing men, but God who tests our hearts.

1 Thessalonians 2:4

Dorothy Sayers once wrote that we are most like God when we create. She meant that when we create something, like a garden, a poem, a needlepoint project, or a rocking chair, we most clearly reflect the image of God in us. When we let ourselves be creative, the Spirit of God and our humanity work together to create beauty. We don't have to be talented to be creative. Of course, its wonderful to be talented at playing the violin or painting landscapes. However, the ability to create goes way beyond talent. Our Creator made each of us to be creative beings. That need to create is internal; it's the way we're put together, regardless of talent. . . .

Christians are called not only to be faithful to our creative passion, art, or craft, but to be faithful to God. Living a creative life is living a faithful life. When we live our passion to create teacups or gardens, God invites us to bring that same creative passion to life with him, a life that never ends.

We can create beauty in everything we do.

ALEXANDRA
STODDARD

HARRIET CROSBY
A Place Called Home

Fear Not, Fret Not

✳

For He Himself has said, "I will never leave you nor forsake you."

H e b r e w s   13 : 5

*W*orry is totally fruitless. Have you ever succeeded in adding an inch where you wanted it, or subtracting one where you didn't want it, merely by being anxious? If you can't accomplish that by worrying, what can you accomplish? . . .

Worry is taking the not-given—for example, tomorrow. Tomorrow is not ours to worry about. We are allowed to plan for tomorrow, but we are not allowed to worry about it. . . .

Worry is refusing the given. Today's care, not tomorrow's, is the responsibility given to us, apportioned in the wisdom of God. . . .

Worry is the antithesis of trust. You simply cannot do both. They are mutually exclusive.

Worry is a wicked squandering of time (as well as energy).

E L I S A B E T H   E L L I O T
Discipline: The Glad Surrender

Walk Straight and Tall

✳

I am the God of your father Abraham; do not fear, for I am with you.

GENESIS 26:24

*I*n my home there are several paintings of women walking toward or into the light. In one, a North African woman is carrying a large bundle on her head. You see her from the back, tall and straight. I like the African way of carrying burdens. The straighter one stands, the more balanced the burden. With all the providing African women do, it's the way they carry the burden that conserves their energy for the important things. No matter how dark the day or heavy their suffering, they balance it with hope and keep on going. . . .

And how to carry burdens, I think now. How to hold on. Go on. Walk on. Straight and tall, to face the dawn with courage.

INGRID TROBISCH
Keeper of the Springs

The secret is Christ in me, not me in a different set of circumstances.

ELISABETH
ELLIOT

✳

*Clouds are God's lace
stretched across the sky.*

ANONYMOUS

There Will Always Be Two

✳

With men this is impossible, but with God all things are possible.

Matthew 19:26

Whatever secrets a new year holds, we will never encounter them alone. There will always be at least two to plow through the tragedies and graciously take the bows. There'll be two to lead the choir and visit the alcoholic. Two to uproot complacency and awaken compassion. Two. Sometimes more, but never less. Christ and you. Christ and me.

We do not wonder if the weeks ahead will surprise or overwhelm Him. We do not wonder whether He will walk into our emergence rooms and cancer centers. . . .

We'll follow Him over the grassy knolls of a family cemetery. We'll lean in to hear His voice amid the heart-wrenching sound of grief.

We question His plans, but not His faithfulness. We pause at His ways, but not His wisdom.

If you want to touch God's heart, use the name he loves to hear. Call him Father.

MAX
LUCADO

JANET PASCAL
The Good Road

Notes

✳

I have found a friend in Jesus
Like no other friend I've known.
When I walk through desert places,
I don't ever walk alone.

JANET   PASCHAL

from "Rock of Ages, Hide Me Again"

_____

_____

_____

_____

_____

_____

_____

_____

_____

_____

_____

_____

_____

_____

_____

_____

Safe and Secure

✳

You alone, O LORD, make me dwell in safety.

P s a l m 4 : 8

We should all sleep like babies every night knowing we are children of the Lord, yet we look to stock portfolios, popularity, jobs, social standing, and other things to give us the security only God can give. We continually construct little emotional bomb shelters, ignoring the more profound gift God offers us, the deep sense that things are all right within us, that in Him we are safe at home.

Trusting in any of our homemade illusions of security instead of the true security of God is idolatry. But, oh, how subtly this one tempts us! If we are realistic at all and read the papers, we see clearly how fragile life is, how fragile we are. We need fortresses against disaster, pain, and loss. We forget that God became a human being with bones that break as easily as ours, with feelings as woundable as ours, and with emotional and physical needs like food, clothes, habitation, friends, and even a town to claim as home.

Trusting God is doing the greatest thing anybody can do.

ELISABETH
ELLIOT

LESLIE WILLIAMS
Seduction of the Lesser Gods

To share a garden is to share a lifetime, past, present, and future. . . . Plants that grew and bloomed in my grandma's garden now grow and bloom in my own garden.

LAURA MARTIN

The Blessing of Daily Bread

❋

Though now you do not see Him, yet believing,
you rejoice with joy inexpressible and full of glory.

1 Peter 1:8

C hicken. Broccoli. Rice. I place another uninspired supper on the dining room table. The house is very quiet. Staring at my plate, I begin to feel just a bit sorry for myself— another meal to eat alone. With a little sigh, I bow my head to say grace. "Lord, for the gift of this food make me truly thankful. Amen." A warm evening breeze moves through the open window. Lifting my head and my fork at the same time, I see Jesus gazing at me with solemn eyes. Before him is a simple earthen platter upon which rests unleavened bread. A small shallow bowl holds a dark-red wine. Jesus raises his as yet unwounded hands in

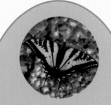

We have access to God's grace, but even more, we have access to Him.

R. C. SPROUL

Week 11

blessing. I understand. The journey is far from over. There is much more to come. More anxious times. More rich blessings. But now, tonight, this supper is ours. And we pray, "Give us this day our daily bread." Amen and amen.

HARRIET CROSBY
A Place Called Home

The green-golding
weeds and grasses have
a gilded look in the
morning sun. They wash
and shine and make their
own soft music.

MARJORIE HOLMES

Lord, Let Me Love

Our Savior Shepherd

✳

The LORD is my shepherd, I shall not want.

PSALM 23:1

This week . . . I have watched the contentment of sheep well fed and well protected on these lush Cotswold pastures where fresh, clear streams flow and where Cotswold-stone fences and thick, tall hedges keep the sheep from wandering and predators from intruding.

And yet as we drove along one narrow, too-well-traveled road, we were startled to go around a curve and see two sheep noses nibbling grass only inches from the roadway They seemed oblivious to the danger. . . . How they needed a shepherd!

How like them we human beings are! When things seem fine from our limited point of view, we may actually be most threatened; because we are so complacent we don't feel a need for a shepherd.

But when we are panicked by life's problems, we may well be safer simple because we are then more aware of our need for a guide, a protector . . . to keep us on the path to a destination we long for but could never find on our own.

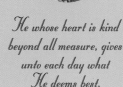

He whose heart is kind beyond all measure, gives unto each day what He deems best.

LINA
SANDELL

✳

GLORIA GAITHER
Because He Lives

Mary's Gift

✳

*Every good gift and every perfect gift is from above,
and comes down from the Father of lights.*

James 1:17

The basic facts are simple and easy to understand. An alabaster jar was a flask made of alabaster stone, itself an object of beauty.

Mary broke it.

Nard from India was a rare perfume kept in its pure form undiluted with less-expensive perfumes. The cost of this perfume could have provided enough bread for 5,000 men and their families. It was worth a year's wages.

Mary emptied it over Jesus. . . .

Mary loved this great teacher. She had seen him kneel to speak to children. Watched him smile and joke. Been filled with awe at the healings he performed. Seen compassion in his every word and touch.

In a patriarchal society where a woman could suffer divorce if her husband disliked her cooking, Jesus was different from other men. He spoke to women, listened to women, included them in his parables, and even taught them—something not allowed in the synagogues.

How could Mary *not* love this man?

SIGMUND BROUWER
The Carpenter's Cloth

The Dignity of a Godly Woman

✳

Lead me in Your truth and teach me,
for You are the God of my salvation.

Psalm 25:5

G od has given woman a uniqueness not found in any other of His creations. . . .

First, God has given women *a special intuition.* This is a sixth sense that allows them to penetrate the hardest shell and see beyond the thickest facade and read the truth beyond error and falsehood. . . .

Second, God has given women *an endurance to pain* that He has not given to most men, whether it is the pain of childbirth, or the ability to handle hardship over the long haul.

Third, . . . God has given women *a unique responsiveness.* We men are far more closed—closed toward God and closed toward one another. But women have an openness, a warmth, a responsive-ness to the things of God. . . .

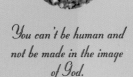

You can't be human and not be made in the image of God.

ELISABETH
ELLIOT

✳

Fourth, God has given women *the quality of vulnerability.* Most women I know are less afraid than men to tell the truth about their lives. . . . Women are willing to ask for help, . . . are less guarded, less defensive They're even willing to admit their fears and apprehensions.

There is a strength of character and an aura of dignity about the godly woman that cannot be found even among godly men.

CHARLES R. SWINDOLL
Esther: A Woman of Strength and Dignity

A garden plot's a healing spot;
I know the feel of sod
Was my dear mother's way to say,
"I've touched a bit of God."

JUNE MASTERS BACHER

Quiet Moments for Women

Paint, Or Get Off the Ladder

✳

Pray without ceasing.

1 THESSALONIANS 5:17

A teenager was given a bucket of paint, a paintbrush, and a ladder, and was told to paint his house. He didn't want to do it, and simply stood on the ladder with all the wherewithal but no action. After a while, his mother came outside and shrieked, "If you don't want to paint, get off the ladder!"

He reminded me of myself—the ladder was like my access to God; the paint, color that I might apply to the dilapidated house of my world; and the paintbrush, the activity of prayer. I have a feeling that sometimes God would like to shout at me, "If you don't want to paint, get off the ladder!" . . .

Why is it that Christians do not pray? I believe it is a matter of the will—a question of *won't* instead of *can't*. . . .

"How do you start to want to?" you may ask. You will need to pray about that! You can't work up the want yourself, and others can't work it up for you. God "will give you your heart's desires" (Psalm 37: 4) if you ask him.

Through prayer we can open a window to God's love.

WARREN MYERS

✳

JILL BRISCOE
Quiet Times with God

Notes

Herein is love;
When I cannot rise to Him
He draws near on wings of grace,
To raise me to Himself.

PURITAN   PRAYER

God Always Answers Prayer

✳

Every morning He brings His justice to light; He never fails.

Zephaniah 3:5

*I*n the process of spiritual development, we are tempted to view prayers answered "yes" as an affirmation of God's love, not realizing that prayer is answered "yes," or "no," or "maybe," or "not yet," or with total silence—and that God loves us no matter what the answer is.

Especially when we pray for something that will make us feel better—for a job, for example, when we're out of work, or for healing, or for a spouse, or for a child—we rejoice when the request is granted. Along with the gift of the job or the spouse itself comes the additional gift, the assurance of God's love. . . . However, when we are praying deep in the night, wrestling with God's silence or with a flat out "no," we don't feel so blessed, or so loved.

Yet, having spent so many nights on my couch, I might argue that we are even more blessed than we realize. Because our need has not been met, because our request has been turned down, we are forced to dig deeper into ourselves and into our relationship with God to uncover the root of the problem. God teaches us the most powerful things through denial.

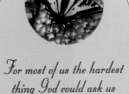

For most of us the hardest thing God could ask us to do is to wait.

GLORIA
GAITHER

✳

LESLIE WILLIAMS
Night Wrestling

The garden looks as
rumpled as clothes left
in the dryer too long.

JUNE MASTERS
BACHER

Pickles and Preservatives

✶

You are the salt of the earth.

Matthew 5:13

Last night, I telephoned the family farm back in Maryland to see how my sister Jay was doing. She was up to her elbows in pickles! Cucumbers are ripe off the vine from Jay's garden so she's spending her evenings boiling and blanching, straining and sealing. I love my sister's pickles, and I think her secret is . . . salt. She adds a lot of salt and tells me that it's the best way to preserve a pickle at its crunchiest, tastiest best.

Those words go well together—salt and preserve. As Christians, we act as a salty preservative in this world, infusing godly values into a life around us. We have the work of restraining evil and advancing good. And just as salt brings out flavor in food, we can "season to taste" our words when the world asks us the reason for the hope that is within us.

> *We treat others as we perceive God is treating us.*
>
> MAX LUCADO
>
> ✶

Week 12

JONI EARECKSON TADA
Diamonds in the Dust

My soul settles in at the sight of the sea! Sea gulls and ships, the smell of fishermen's nets drying in the sun, the mist moving like a lady in her chiffon evening gown across the harbor.

GLORIA GAITHER

We Have This Moment

My Portion and My Cup

✳

But the Lord is faithful, who will establish you and guard you from the evil one.

2 Thessalonians 3:3

A quiet heart is content with what God gives. It is enough. All is grace. One morning my computer simply would not obey me. What a nuisance. I had my work laid out, my timing figured, my mind all set. My work was delayed, my timing thrown off, my thinking interrupted. Then I remembered. It was not for nothing. This was part of the Plan (not mine, His). "Lord, You have assigned me my portion and my cup."

Now if the interruption had been a human being instead of an infuriating mechanism, it would not have been so hard to see it as the most important part of the work of the day. But *all* is under my Father's control: yes, recalcitrant computers, faulty transmissions, drawbridges which happen to be up when one is in a hurry. My portion. My cup. My lot is secure. My heart can be at peace. My Father is in charge. How simple!

Our Savior is the harbor of weather-beaten sails.

CHARLES SPURGEON

ELISABETH ELLIOT
Keep a Quiet Heart

Simple Solitude

✳

*You are complete in Him, who is the head
of all principality and power.*

Colossians 2:10

I [am] surrounded by the stark, white walls of a small lodging room at Shaker Village of Pleasant Hill, Kentucky. . . .

The straight edges of Shaker furniture say, "Welcome to a place where beauty is found in a straight line." . . .

The horizontal band of pegs that ring the room say, "Welcome to a place of order." . . .

The sparse furnishings say, "Welcome to a place where you can breathe." . . .

The Shaker silence, broken only by a softly closed door or faint step in the hall, says, "Welcome to a place of solitude." . . .

Suddenly, the pieces of the Shaker puzzle come together: It is a prayer closet! Each room is created with as few distractions as possible, so that at any moment one might kneel on the hard floor and find God, waiting in the silence, saying, "We make you kindly welcome."

LIZ CURTIS HIGGS
Reflecting His Image

Bumps and Jolts Along the Way

✳

"I will be a Father to you, and you shall be My
sons and daughters," says the LORD Almighty.

2 CORINTHIANS 6:18

*T*he path by which God takes us often seems to lead away from our good, causing us to believe we've missed a turn and taken the wrong road. That's because most of us have been taught to believe that if we're on the right track God's goodness will always translate into earthly good: that He'll heal, deliver, and exempt us from disease and pain; that we'll have money in the bank, kids who turn out well, nice clothes, a comfortable living, and a leisurely retirement. . . .

Your life has been appointed by God's wise providence.

F. B. MEYER

But that's a pipe dream far removed from the biblical perspective that God's love often leads us down roads where earthly comforts fail us so He can give us eternal consolation. . .

God doesn't cushion the journey; He lets life jolt us. . . . As F. B. Meyer said, if we've been told that we're supposed to be on a bumpy track, every jolt along the way simply confirms the fact that we're still on the right road.

DAVID ROPER
Psalm 23

*Though we travel the
world over to find the
beautiful,
we must carry it with us
or we find it not.*

RALPH WALDO
EMERSON

Lord, Keep Me at It

✳

Through love, serve one another.

Galatians 5:13

God, give me due respect for the abilities you have given me.

Don't let me sell them short. Don't let me cheapen them. Don't let me bury my talents through indecision, cowardice, or laziness. . . .

Give me the energy, strength, and will power to bring your gifts to their proper fruition. Keep me at it. . . .

When friends laugh at me, keep me at it.

When people tempt me away from it, keep me at it.

When others scorn what I have produced, let me not be discouraged. Keep me at it. . . .

Let nothing really matter but these precious gifts you have entrusted to me. For their sake let me be willing and proud to make the sacrifice. Keep me at it.

MARJORIE HOLMES
Lord Let Me Love

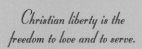

Christian liberty is the freedom to love and to serve.

LUCILLE
SOLLENBERGER

✳

$\mathcal{N}otes$

As the years pass, I am coming more and more to understand that it is the common, everyday blessings of our common everyday lives for which we should be particularly grateful.

LAURA INGALLS WILDER

Tending the Inner Garden

✳

It is no longer I who live, but Christ lives in me.

Galatians 2:20

The goal is spiritual balance, an impossible feat to manage unless we continually tend the inner garden with prayer, tossing distractions back over the wall as they invade our privacy. If we scurry about, doing God's work in the world without time for reflection, then we get out of sorts with ourselves, our children, and the people to whom we're trying to minister. When my life is crowded, I resent grading papers, I do not have time to play Candyland, and dinner comes out of a box. That I am doing the "work of the Lord" is slim consolation when I don't even have time to say hello to my Maker, or to watch and listen to what He is trying to show me through each item on a hastily crossed-off list.

The great temptation is to think that an unbalanced life is not a serious problem, and not a life-threatening disease. Big mistake.

LESLIE WILLIAMS
Night Wrestling

Lord take me to the cross and leave me there.

PURITAN
PRAYER

✳

I can remember vividly the
sun passing through the
emerald green cathedral of
a weeping willow and
illuminating the sandy
bottom of the riverbed
with the fire of a thousand
minute diamonds.

MADELEINE
KAMMAN

*When French
Women Cook*

Singing Birds of the Heart

* ❋ *

*God is able to make all grace abound toward you, that you
. . . may have an abundance for every good work.*

2 Corinthians 9:8

*I*f I keep a green bough in my heart,
the singing bird will come," says an
ancient Chinese proverb. If our
hearts wore "Welcome" signs, what
birds might we attract?

Perhaps the first bird to arrive would
be that of *Kindness.* A song of kindness
comes from a heart filled with love. It
does not long for a larger limb where it
can do great things. It sings a song of
kindness in its own little green bough; and
that is true greatness.

*True worship will inevitably
find expression in loving,
sacrificial service.*

J. OSWALD
SANDERS

❋

Would you suppose the next guest might be the
bird of *Enthusiasm?* Enthusiasm sings with a sparkle in its eye. It
sings of the zest of life. It sings of faith, hope, and charity—never
complaining about its job,
but ever begging for more
work to do.

And here comes the bird of
Generosity! It shares its song—with or without talent. It loves and
is loved because its secret is happiness. Its song is so service-filled
that all doors open to hear its words.

Week 13

JUNE MASTERS BACHER

Quiet Moments for Women

When the hot afternoon
sun shimmers across
the earth, humankind
and the beasts of the
field all settle down in
shaded depths, to sleep,
to catch a wayward
breeze, or to watch a
hawk becalmed in a
cloudless azure sky.

JANE WATSON
HOPPING

*The Lazy Days of
Summer Cookbook*

Everyday Blessings

✳

Daily blessing: Let all that you do be done with love.

1 Corinthians 16:14

E ach day, each moment is so pregnant with eternity
that if we "tune in" to it, we can hardly contain
the joy. I have a feeling this is what happened
to Moses when he saw the burning bush. Maybe
Yahweh performed laser surgery on his eyes so
he could see what was always there, and Moses
was just so overwhelmed with the "glory" of
God that the very ground he stood on became
infused with "holiness" and the bushes along the
mountain path burned with splendor. Whatever
happened, the burning bush experience also
sharpened Moses' awareness of the pain of his
people in the light of God's presence. . . .

Pain and pleasure, laughter and tears are all around
us, too, if we can see them and respond to them. . . .

God has given us this day. I don't want to miss it. . . . Enjoy!

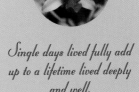

*Single days lived fully add
up to a lifetime lived deeply
and well.*

ALEXANDRA
STODDARD

GLORIA GAITHER
Because He Lives

Christ Redeems the Crummy Stuff

✳

*Whatever things were written before were written for
our learning, that we through the patience and
comfort of the Scriptures might have hope.*

Romans 15:4

When we give ourselves *to* Christ, He redeems all the crummy stuff life tries to defeat us with. . . .

Though it is our fingers that do the dialing and we who have to deal with the frustrations of expensive electricians, plumbers who run four hours late, or whatever else has gone wrong, Jesus helps us from the inside. He gives us patience, He soothes our irritated spirits, He even leads us to ways we can, after all, afford the repairs. . . .

I picture Jesus in a worker's apron standing behind a counter in a shop cluttered with bits and pieces of all of life's junk. A sign above the fix-it shop's door says, "Welcome. Open twenty -four hours a day. Will give you patience and inspiration to help heal everything from broken washing machines to broken hearts. May take longer than expected. Situation may not look as you originally planned. But redemption of some sort guaranteed."

LESLIE WILLIAMS
Seduction of the Lesser Gods

In the Living Room of God's Heart

✳

*For of Him and through Him and to Him
are all things, to whom be glory forever.*

ROMANS 11:36

or too long we have been in a far country: a
country of noise and hurry and crowds, a
country of climb and push and shove, a
country of frustration and fear and intimidation. And
[God] welcomes us home: home to serenity and
peace and joy, home to friendship and fellowship
and openness, home to intimacy and acceptance
and affirmation.

*God comes not questwise to
His saints' house, but
to dwell with them.*

GURNALL

We do not need to be shy. He invites us into the
living room of his heart, where we can put on old
slippers and share freely. He invites us into the
kitchen of his friendship, where chatter and batter mix
in good fun. He invites us into the dining room of his
strength, where we can feast to our heart's delight. He
invites us into the study of his wisdom, where we can learn and
grow and stretch . . . and ask all the questions we want. He
invites us into the workshop of his creativity, where we can
be co-laborers with him, working together to determine the
outcomes of events. He invites us into the bedroom of his rest,
where new peace is found and where we can be naked and
vulnerable and free. It is also the place of deepest intimacy,
where we know and are known to the fullest.

RICHARD J. FOSTER
Finding the Heart's True Home

God made gardens to
delight our human
senses.

HARRIET CROSBY

An Ordinary Path

✳

Let us hold fast the confession of our hope without
wavering, for He who promised is faithful.

H e b r e w s   1 0 : 2 3

T hroughout the history of the church, men
and women have been called to make their
journey along "a way they do not know."
Moses finally got his people to the Promised
Land, only to discover that the land of milk and
honey also overflowed with giants. Although
Augustine, in his heart of hearts, was drawn to
God, still he prayed, "Lord, make me chaste—but
not yet." St. John of the Cross agonized through
the dark night of the soul. Brother Lawrence, even
while practicing the presence of God, still had his
pots and pans to scrub.

The journey of the spirit is not a highway for saints
and mystics, but an ordinary path laid out for ordinary
people. All of us have a call to answer; all of us have a road of
faith to walk. And while each of us has individual stumbling
points and places of darkness, we share in a single truth: that the
process is of supreme importance to the Lord. And the process
of moving from religion to reality is a way that leads to true
intimacy with God.

The quest for a simpler life
is itself an infinite journey
toward God.

WANDA
URBANSKA

PENELOPE J. STOKES
Faith: The Substance of Things Unseen

Notes

Life is mostly what we make it,
Filled with sunshine or with storm;
Just whichever way we take it—
Sad or cheering—cold or warm.

ANONYMOUS

The Seasons of God's Care

✴

For it is God . . . who has shone in our hearts to give
the light of the knowledge of the glory of God.

2 Corinthians 4:6

Without the changing seasons, vineyards would never bear fruit. Each season offers some-thing the vine needs for continued growth. Spring brings rain and softened days to gently stimulate the growth that will come to full maturity in the vibrant warmth of summer. Autumn is the time of harvest, and winter brings a much-needed rest and restaging to the vine. Without this rest, the vine would not be strong enough to go through the cycle again to harvest. . . .

*We need to live in the light
of His countenance daily.*

ANDREW
MURRAY

✴

Likewise, our spiritual growth demands an ever-changing climate—seasons when God's work is tailor-made to our personal circumstances. Seasons designed by the Father as he nourishes our lives toward fruitfulness. Seasons that bring a healthy balance of joy and challenge, of diligent effort and renewing rest.

We must learn not only to embrace the season we're in, to enjoy its gifts and confront its challenges, but also to let it go when the seasons change.

WAYNE JACOBSEN
In My Father's Vineyard

Acknowledgments

✳

*Grateful acknowledgment is made to the following
publishers and copyright holders for permission
to reprint copyrighted material.*

June Masters Bacher, *Quiet Moments for Women* (Eugene, Or.: Harvest House, 1979).

June Masters Bacher, *The Quiet Heart* (Eugene, Or.: Harvest House, 1988).

Jill Briscoe, *Quiet Times with God,* (Wheaton, Ill: Tyndale House, 1997).

Sigmund Brouwer, *The Carpenter's Cloth* (Nashville: Word Inc., 1998). All rights reserved.

Harriet Crosby, *A Well-Watered Garden* (Nashville: Thomas Nelson, 1995).

Harriet Crosby, *A Place Called Home* (Nashville, Thomas Nelson, 1997).

Elisabeth Elliot, *The Path of Loneliness* (Nashville: Thomas Nelson,

Elisabeth Elliot, *Keep a Quiet Heart* (Ann Arbor, Mich.: Servant Books, 1995).

Elisabeth Elliot, *God's Guidance* (Grand Rapids: Fleming H. Revell, 1997).

Elisabeth Elliot: *Discipline, The Glad Surrender* (Grand Rapids: Fleming H. Revell, 1982).

Suzanne Dale Ezell, *Living Simply in God's Abundance* (Nashville: Thomas Nelson, 1998).

Richard J. Foster, *Finding the Heart's True Home* (San Francisco: HerperCollins, 1992).

Gloria Gaither, *Because He Lives* (Grand Rapids: Zondervan, 1997). Used by permission.

Ken Gire, *Windows of the Soul* (Grand Rapids: Zondervan, 1996).

Liz Curtis Higgs, *Reflecting His Image* (Nashville: Thomas Nelson, 1996).

Marjorie Holmes, *Lord, Let Me Love* (New York: Bantam Doubleday Dell, 1978). ©Marjorie Holmes.

Wayne Jacobsen, *In My Father's Vineyard* (Dallas: Word, 1997).

Margaret Jensen, *Papa's Place* (Eugene, OR.: Harvest House, 1998.

Barbara Johnson, *Joy Breaks* (Grand Rapids: Zondervan, 1997). Used by permission.

Phillip Keller, *Songs of My Soul* (Dallas: Word, 1989).

Phillip Keller, *Taming Tension* (Grand Rapids: Baker Book House, 1979). ©Phillip Keller.

Anne Graham Lotz, *The Vision of His Glory* (Dallas: Word, 1996).

Janet Paschal, *The Good Road* (Sisters, Or.: Multnomah Books, 1997).

David Roper, *Psalm 23: Hope and Rest from the Shepherd* (Grand Rapids: Discovery House, 1994). Used by permission of Discovery House Publishers, Box 3566, Grand Rapids, MI 49501. All rights reserved.

David Roper, *Elijah: A Man Like Us* (Grand Rapids: Discovery House, 1997). Used by permission of Discovery House Publishers, Box 3566, Grand Rapids, MI 49501. All rights reserved.

Edith Schaeffer, *What Is a Family?* (Grand Rapids, Mich.: Baker Book House, 1975).

Sara Wenger Shenk, *Coming Home* (Intercourse, Penn.: Good Books, 1992).

Soul Searching: Meditations for Your Spiritual Journey (Nashville: Thomas Nelson, 1995).

Penelope J. Stokes, *Faith: The Substance of Things Unseen* (Wheaton: Tyndale, 1995). ©Penelope J. Stokes

Charles R. Swindoll, *Esther: A Woman of Strength and Dignity* (Nashville: Word, 1997).

Charles R. Swindoll, *David: A Man of Passion and Destiny* (Dallas: Word, 1997).

Joni Eareckson Tada, *Diamonds in the Dust* (Grand Rapids; Zondervan, 1993). Used by permission.

Ingrid Trobisch, *Keeper of the Springs* (Sisters, Or.: Multnomah Gift Books, A Division of Multnomah Publishers, Inc., 1997).

Peter Wallace, *What the Psalmist Is Saying to You Today* (Nashville: Thomas Nelson, 1995).

Sheila Walsh, *Gifts for Your Soul* (Grand Rapids: Zondervan, 1997). Used by permission.

Leslie Williams, *Night Wrestling* (Dallas: Word, 1997).

Leslie Williams, *Seduction of the Lesser Gods* (Dallas: Word, 1998).

Photo Credits

✹

COVER
Rita Maas Photography

INTERIOR
Steve Terrill Photography, Portland, Oregon.